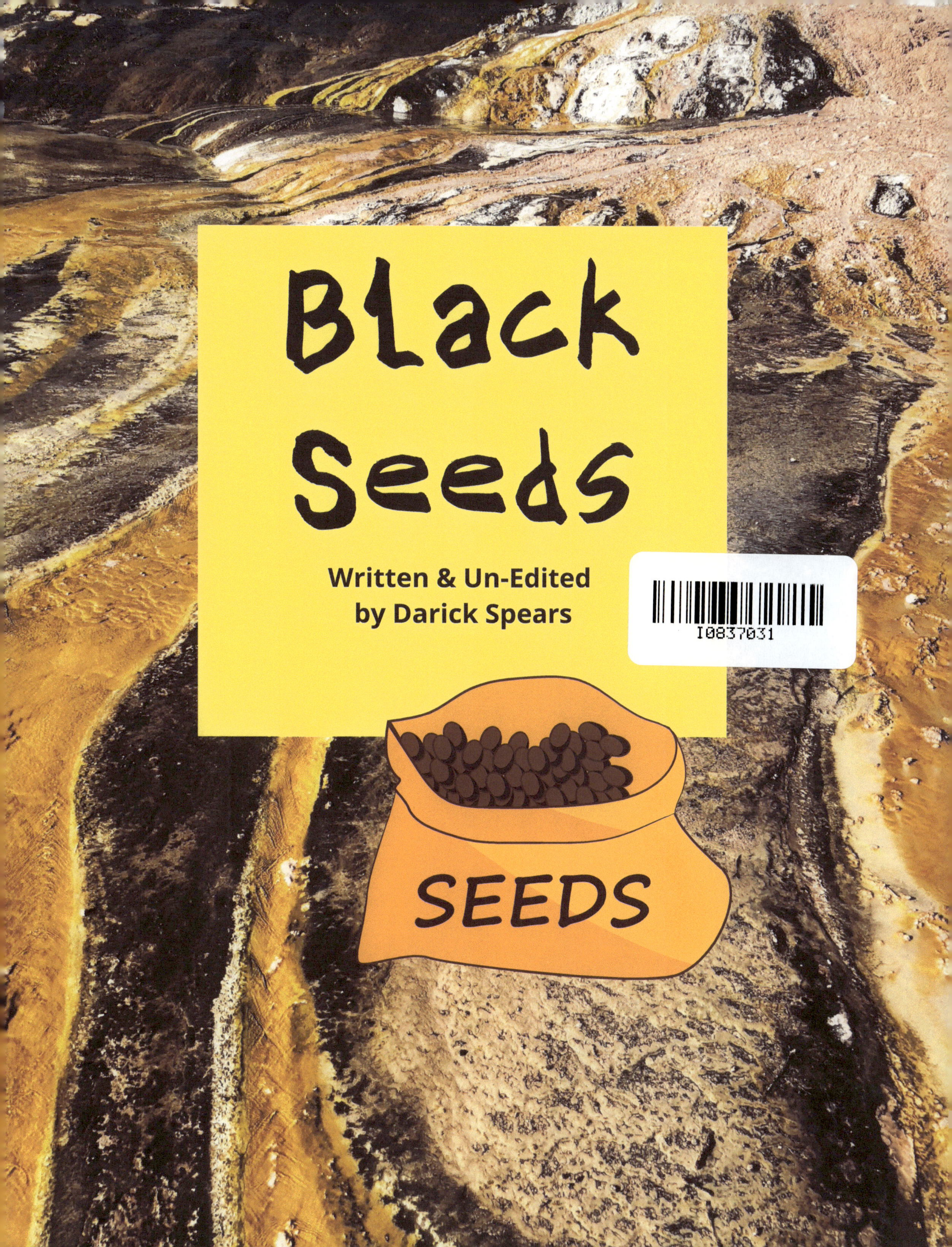
Black Seeds
Written & Un-Edited
by Darick Spears
SEEDS

BLACK SEEDS

ISBN: 978-1-954133-12-9

DARICK BOOKS

PUBLISHED THROUGH
DARICK BOOKS
DDS MEDIAWORKS LLC./21ST CENTURY SHAKESPEARS PUBLISHING
WWW.DARICKBOOKS.COM

GET YOUR BOOK WRITTEN & PUBLISHED TODAY
BY

DARICK SPEARS
EMAIL: DARICK@DDSMEDIAWORKS.COM
CALL 414-988-4946

THEY MANAGE TO GROW EVEN ON
THE UNSOILED GROUNDS,
CLASSIFIED AS STAINS ON THE
LAND BUT THEY MANAGE TO
ELEVATE AND BECOME PROFOUND.
I CALL THEM BLACK SEEDS,
THE FIRST GENERATION.
BUT HAVE THEY BEEN TRICKED BY
THE SNARES OF SATAN?
HAS HE STOLEN THEIR WORTH?

TELL ME NO LIES,
ONLY THE TRUTH.
THE REVOLUTION MAY NEVER BE
TELEVISED,
BE AWARE OF THE REPORTERS
THAT ARE PAID TO REPORT LIES.
THOSE LIES OF COURSE, ARE TOLD
TO YOU!

EACH DAY TWO SEEDS ARE
THROWN ONTO THE GROUND.
ONE WILL DIE AND THE OTHER
MAY SURVIVE.
BLACK SEEDS HAVE ALWAYS
HAD LIMITED RESOURCES,
YET THEY ALWAYS FIND A WAY TO
PROPAGATE.

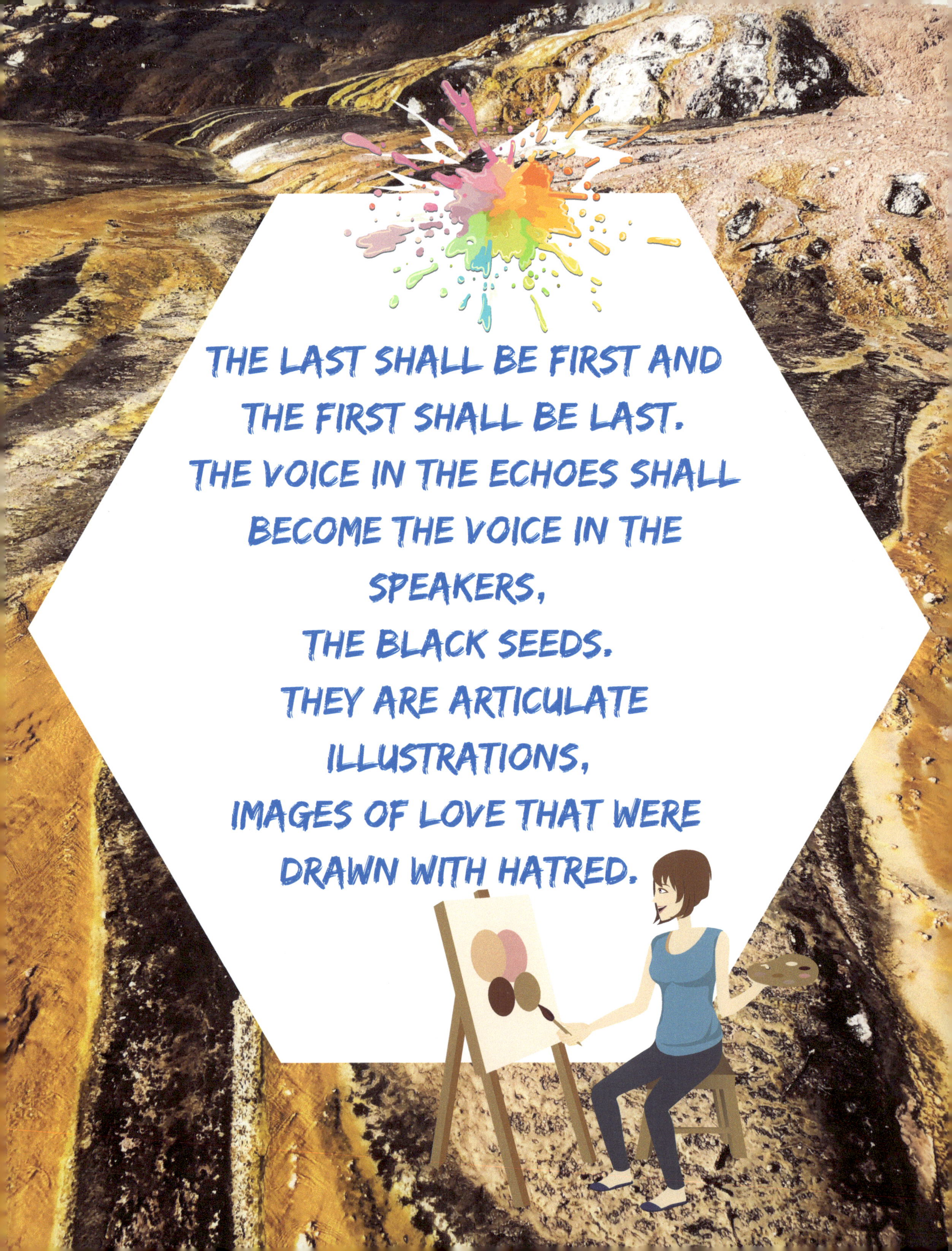
THE LAST SHALL BE FIRST AND
THE FIRST SHALL BE LAST.
THE VOICE IN THE ECHOES SHALL
BECOME THE VOICE IN THE
SPEAKERS,
THE BLACK SEEDS.
THEY ARE ARTICULATE
ILLUSTRATIONS,
IMAGES OF LOVE THAT WERE
DRAWN WITH HATRED.

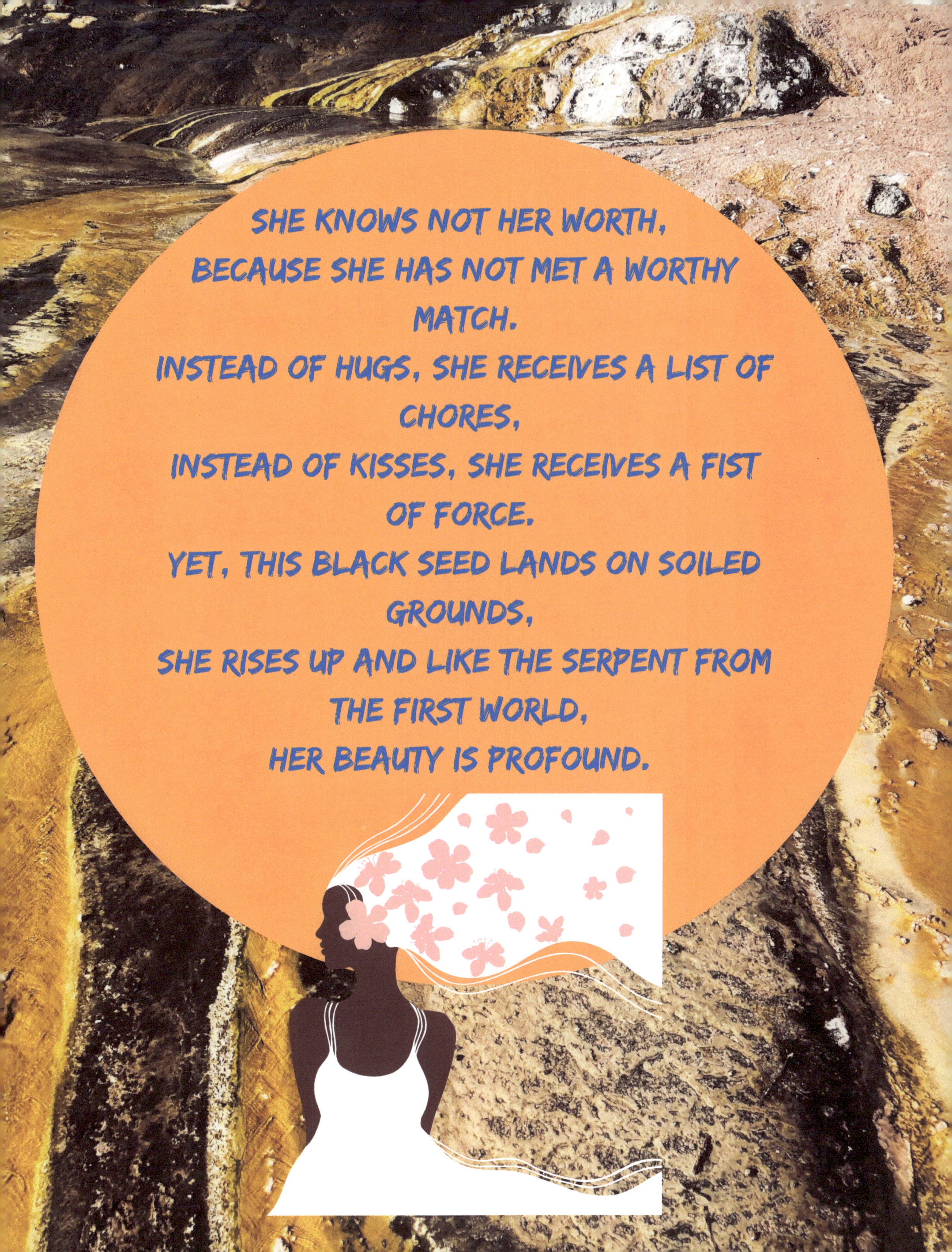
SHE KNOWS NOT HER WORTH,
BECAUSE SHE HAS NOT MET A WORTHY MATCH.
INSTEAD OF HUGS, SHE RECEIVES A LIST OF CHORES,
INSTEAD OF KISSES, SHE RECEIVES A FIST OF FORCE.
YET, THIS BLACK SEED LANDS ON SOILED GROUNDS,
SHE RISES UP AND LIKE THE SERPENT FROM THE FIRST WORLD,
HER BEAUTY IS PROFOUND.

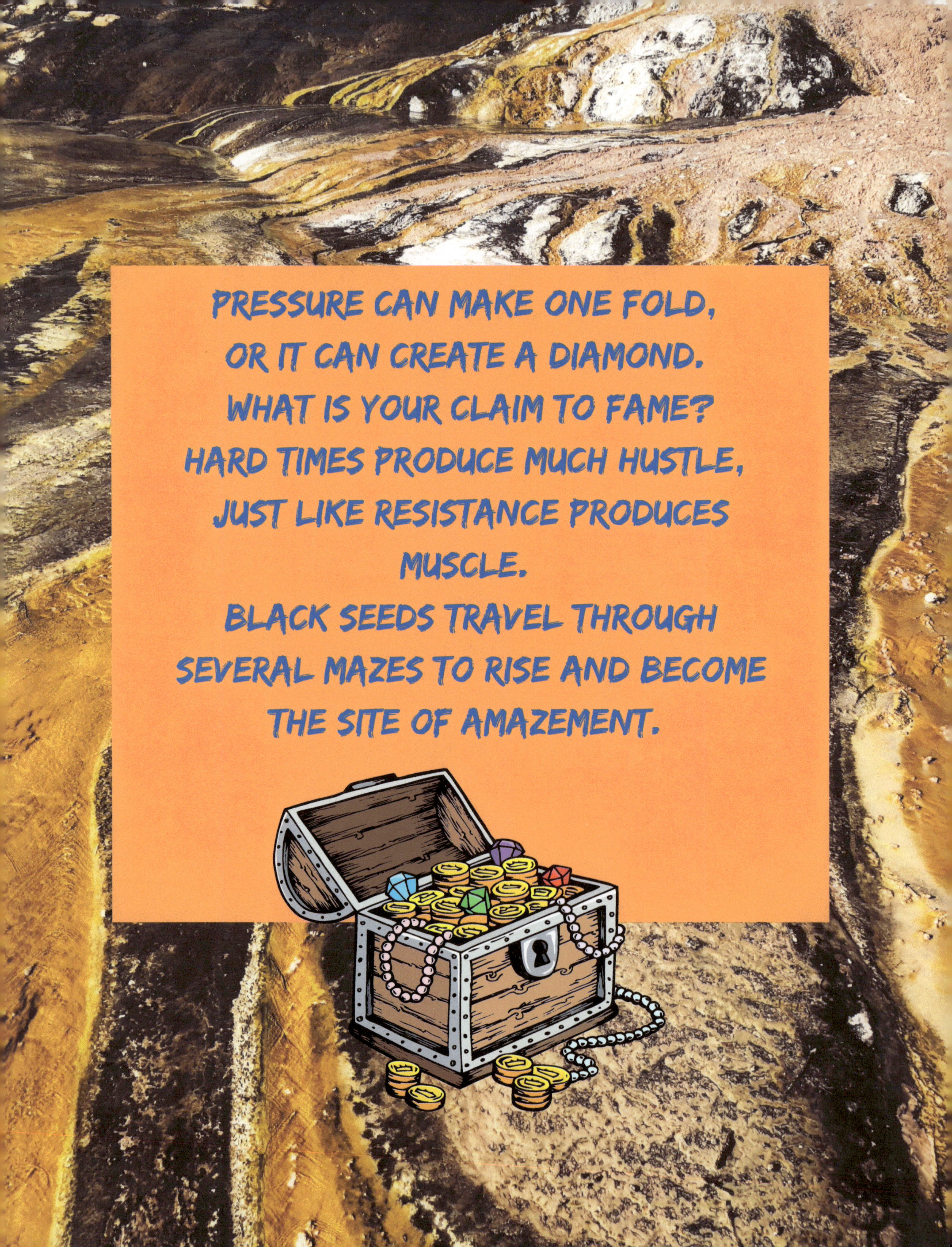
PRESSURE CAN MAKE ONE FOLD,
OR IT CAN CREATE A DIAMOND.
WHAT IS YOUR CLAIM TO FAME?
HARD TIMES PRODUCE MUCH HUSTLE,
JUST LIKE RESISTANCE PRODUCES
MUSCLE.
BLACK SEEDS TRAVEL THROUGH
SEVERAL MAZES TO RISE AND BECOME
THE SITE OF AMAZEMENT.

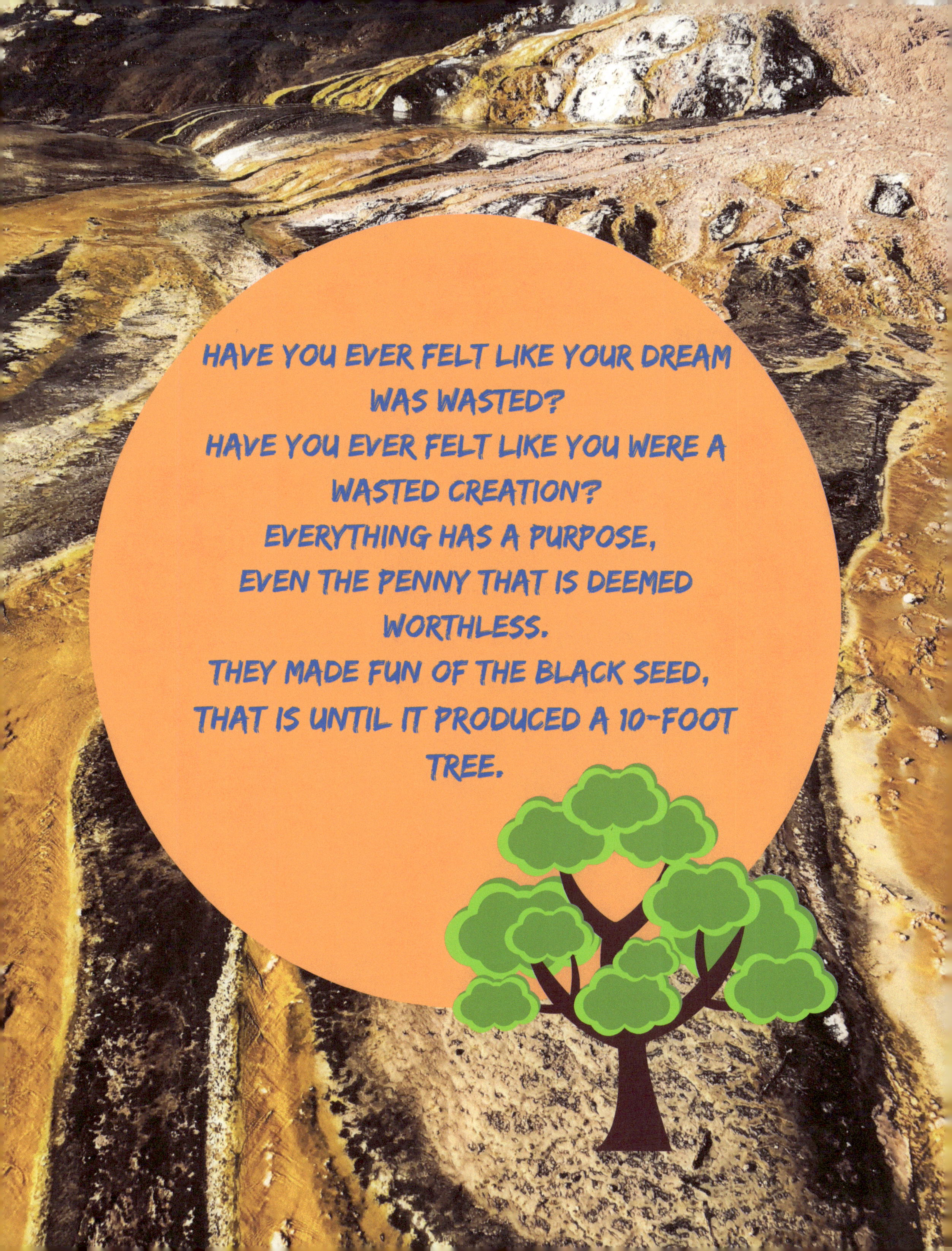
HAVE YOU EVER FELT LIKE YOUR DREAM
WAS WASTED?
HAVE YOU EVER FELT LIKE YOU WERE A
WASTED CREATION?
EVERYTHING HAS A PURPOSE,
EVEN THE PENNY THAT IS DEEMED
WORTHLESS.
THEY MADE FUN OF THE BLACK SEED,
THAT IS UNTIL IT PRODUCED A 10-FOOT
TREE.

THAT TREE IS "ME,"
THAT TREE IS "WE."
THE BLACK SEEDS ARE THE SALT OF THE EARTH,
THE VICTIMS THAT BECAME THE VICTORS.
THE ROSES THAT CRACKED OPEN THE CONCRETE.
SPROUTING INTO EXISTENCE AND BECOMING A MAINSTAY.

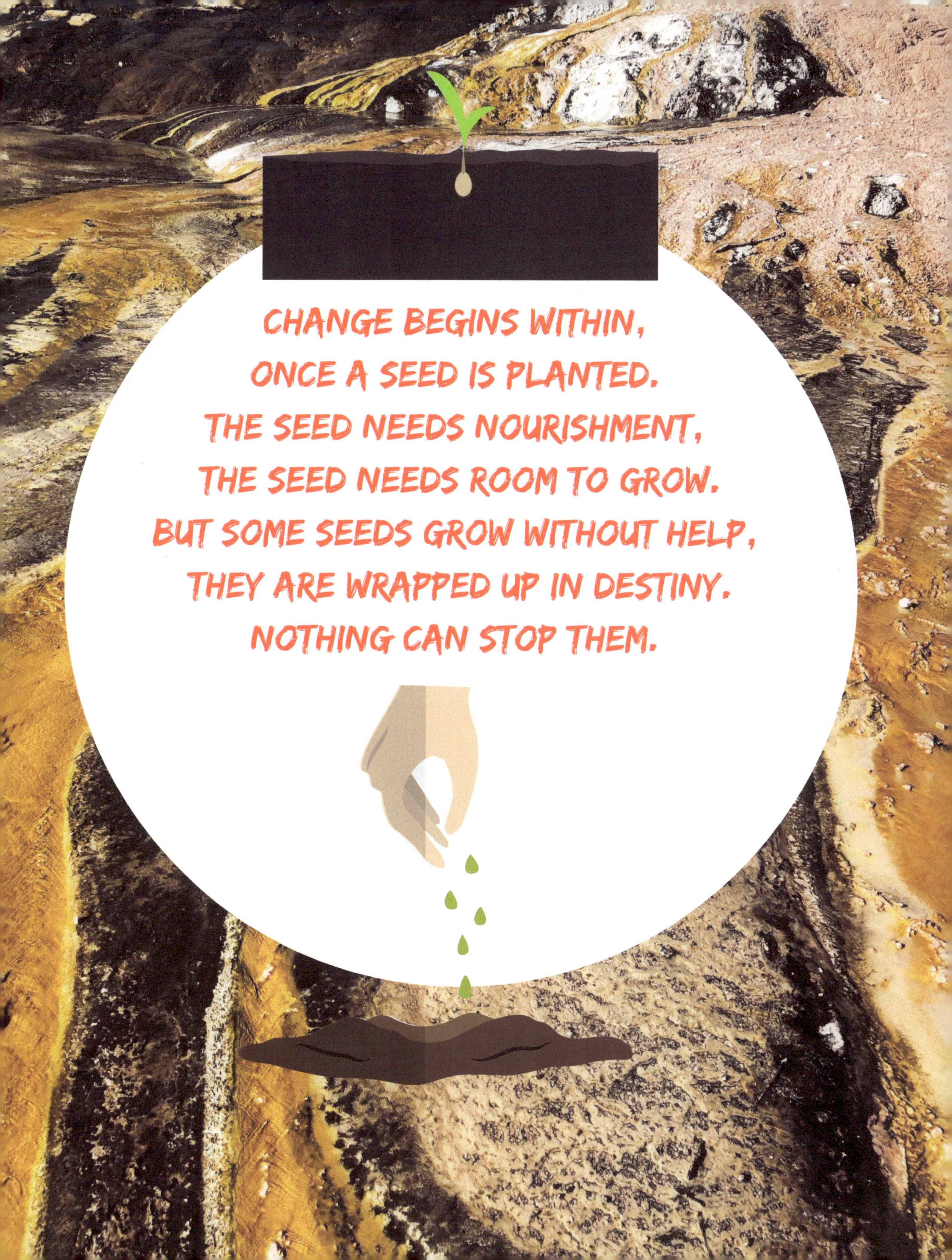
CHANGE BEGINS WITHIN,
ONCE A SEED IS PLANTED.
THE SEED NEEDS NOURISHMENT,
THE SEED NEEDS ROOM TO GROW.
BUT SOME SEEDS GROW WITHOUT HELP,
THEY ARE WRAPPED UP IN DESTINY.
NOTHING CAN STOP THEM.

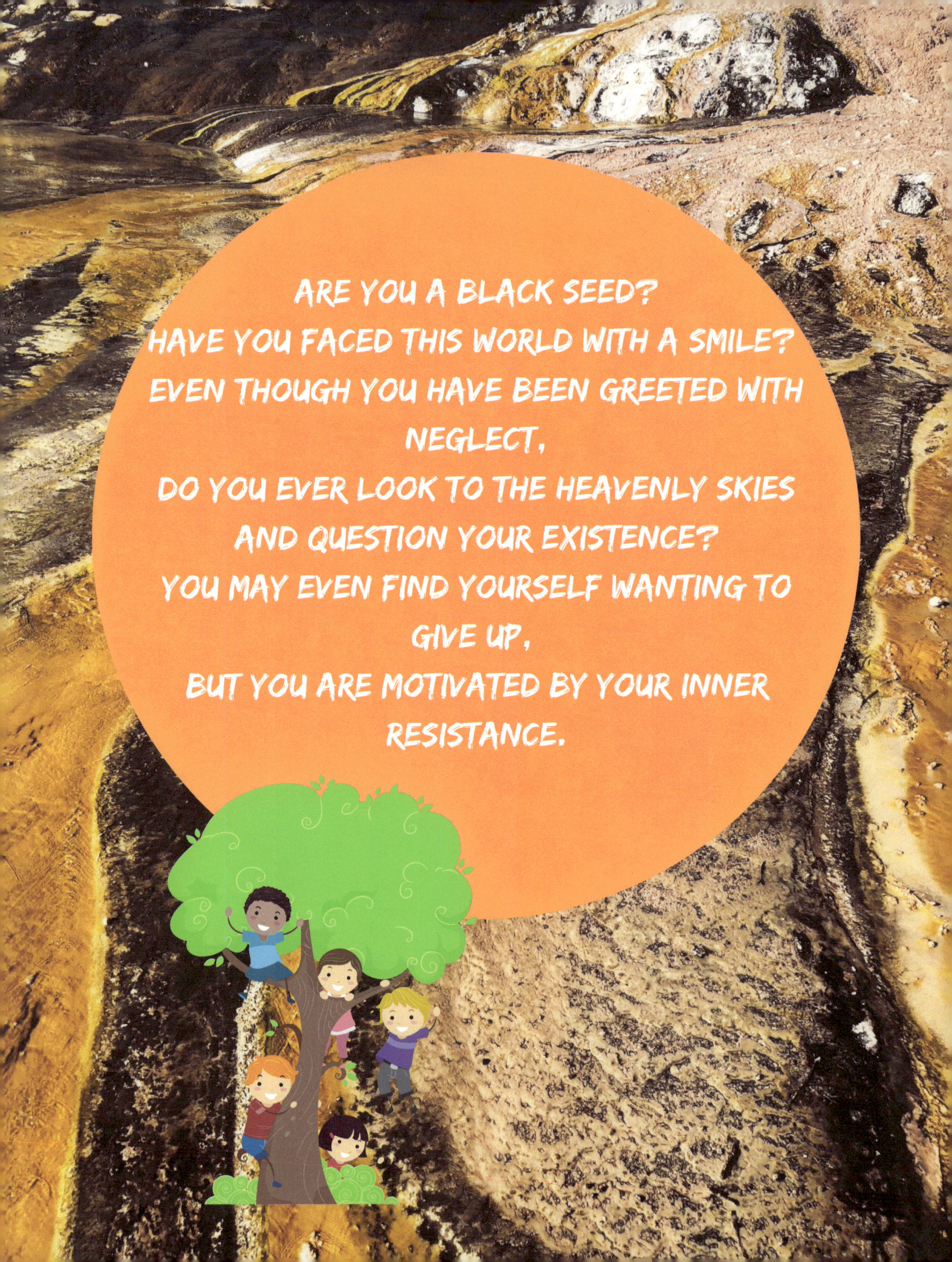
ARE YOU A BLACK SEED?
HAVE YOU FACED THIS WORLD WITH A SMILE?
EVEN THOUGH YOU HAVE BEEN GREETED WITH NEGLECT,
DO YOU EVER LOOK TO THE HEAVENLY SKIES
AND QUESTION YOUR EXISTENCE?
YOU MAY EVEN FIND YOURSELF WANTING TO GIVE UP,
BUT YOU ARE MOTIVATED BY YOUR INNER RESISTANCE.

SOCIETY PARALYZES THOSE WHO ARE DIFFERENT.
THAT IS PART OF THE CRIPPLING SYSTEM.
BLACK SEEDS,
I HURT JUST LIKE THE NEXT PERSON,
I CRY MYSELF TO SLEEP AT NIGHT.
FEELING SO INSECURE EVEN IN THE ARMS OF SECURITY.
BEGGING GOD FOR REASONS OF MY EXISTENCE.

BLACK SEEDS,
I BELIEVE THAT THE GOOD LORD JESUS
MADE US IN HIS IMAGE,
BLACK SEEDS.
HE WAS DESPISED AND REJECTED,
CRUCIFIED AND YET HE ROSE.
WE CANNOT BE STOPPED JUST LIKE
THE TICKING OF LIFE'S CLOCK.

DARK DAYTIMES,
SLEEPNESS OWL HOURS.
COLD SUMMER WINDS,
HOT WINTER FLURRIES.
UNSOILED GROUNDS,
METICULOUS DETAILS -- ALL
DESCRIBING THE DEVELOPMENT OF THE
BLACK SEED.

SLAVERY,
A MIND-STATE,
A TIME FRAME,
A BLIND DATE.
ONCE AN EYE IS GIVEN SIGHT,
IT IS NO LONGER A SLAVE.
IT IS FREE TO VIEW THE WORLD AS IT IS.
RISE AND WAKE UP MY FELLOW BLACK SEEDS.
LET MY WORDS GIVE YOU LIFE.

MENTAL RESURRECTION,
PHYSICAL REDEMPTION.
FOR THE BLACK SEED WAS MEANT
TO RISE ON ANY GROUND IT
EMBRACED.
NOTHING CAN CURSE THAT WHICH IS
BLESSED.
WHEN ONE TAKES FLIGHT,
THE OTHERS PREPARE FOR COMBAT.
WATCH THOSE YOU KEEP CLOSE.

WITH MY WORDS, I PLANT INSIDE
EACH READER A SEED,
ONE DAY IT WILL GROW.
BE THE HOPE AND NOT THE
HOPELESS,
BE THE VOICE AND NOT THE
VOICELESS.
THERE ARE LEVELS IN LIFE,
AND THERE ARE DEVILS IN LIGHT.
BE CAUTIOUS.

BE OPEN TO CHANGE,
BUT CLOSED-MINDED TO BEING
STAGNANT.
THE SEED IS POWERFUL ONCE IT
BEGINS TO GROW.
LET GOD BE YOUR NOURISHMENT,
LET LOVE BE YOUR ROOTS,
AND LET ASTONISHMENT BE YOUR
PORTRAIT.
Color Pencils
NOTE BOOK

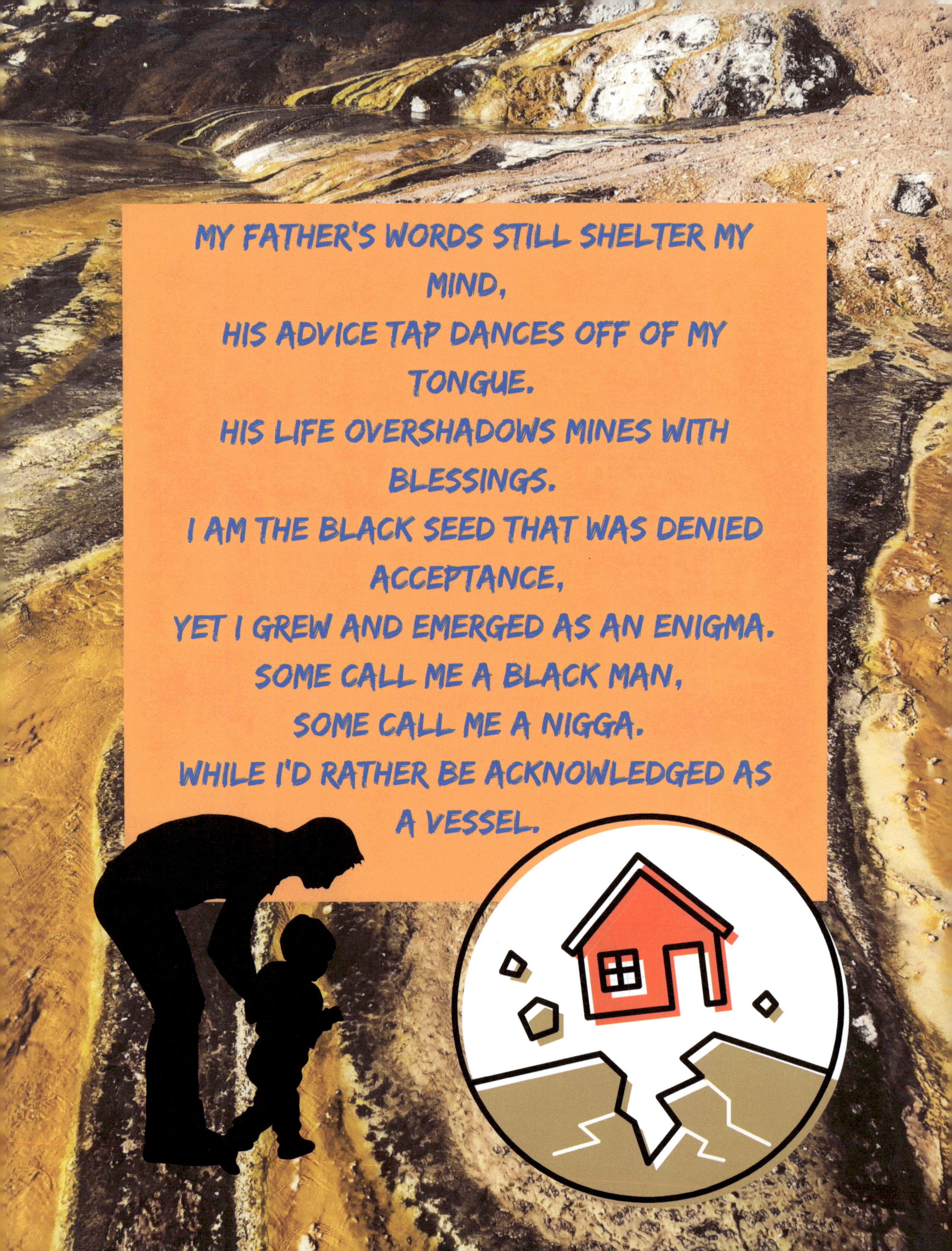
MY FATHER'S WORDS STILL SHELTER MY MIND,
HIS ADVICE TAP DANCES OFF OF MY TONGUE.
HIS LIFE OVERSHADOWS MINES WITH BLESSINGS.
I AM THE BLACK SEED THAT WAS DENIED ACCEPTANCE,
YET I GREW AND EMERGED AS AN ENIGMA.
SOME CALL ME A BLACK MAN,
SOME CALL ME A NIGGA.
WHILE I'D RATHER BE ACKNOWLEDGED AS A VESSEL.

I CAME FROM THE EYE OF THE TORNADO,
AND I LANDED SAFELY ON UNSETTLED
GROUNDS.
BUT I ROSE TO BE A FIRM FOUNDATION
FOR THOSE AROUND ME.
I SWAM BRAVELY WITHIN THE WATERS
THAT WERE SUPPOSED TO DROWN ME.
AND HERE I AM.
SEEDS

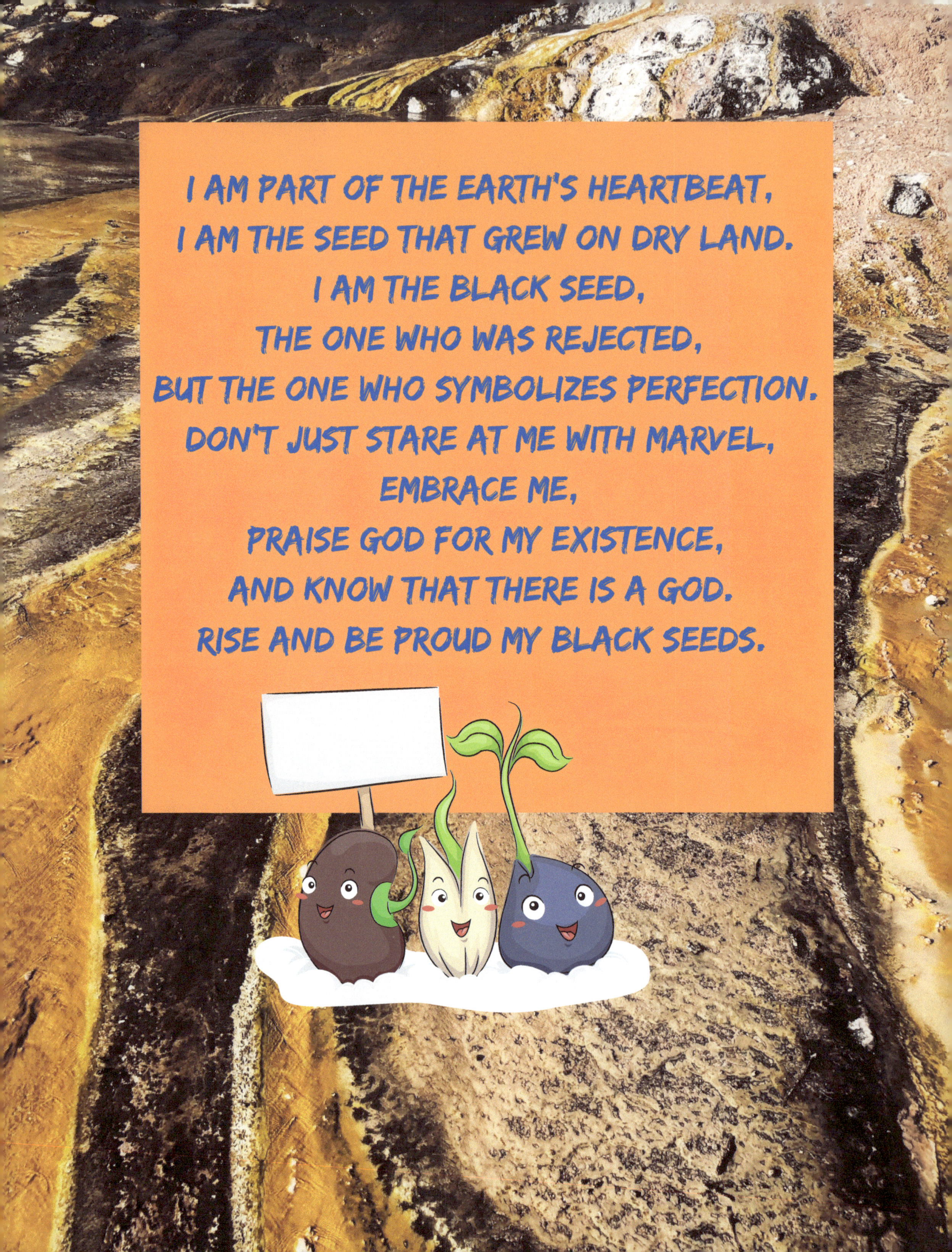
I AM PART OF THE EARTH'S HEARTBEAT,
I AM THE SEED THAT GREW ON DRY LAND.
I AM THE BLACK SEED,
THE ONE WHO WAS REJECTED,
BUT THE ONE WHO SYMBOLIZES PERFECTION.
DON'T JUST STARE AT ME WITH MARVEL,
EMBRACE ME,
PRAISE GOD FOR MY EXISTENCE,
AND KNOW THAT THERE IS A GOD.
RISE AND BE PROUD MY BLACK SEEDS.

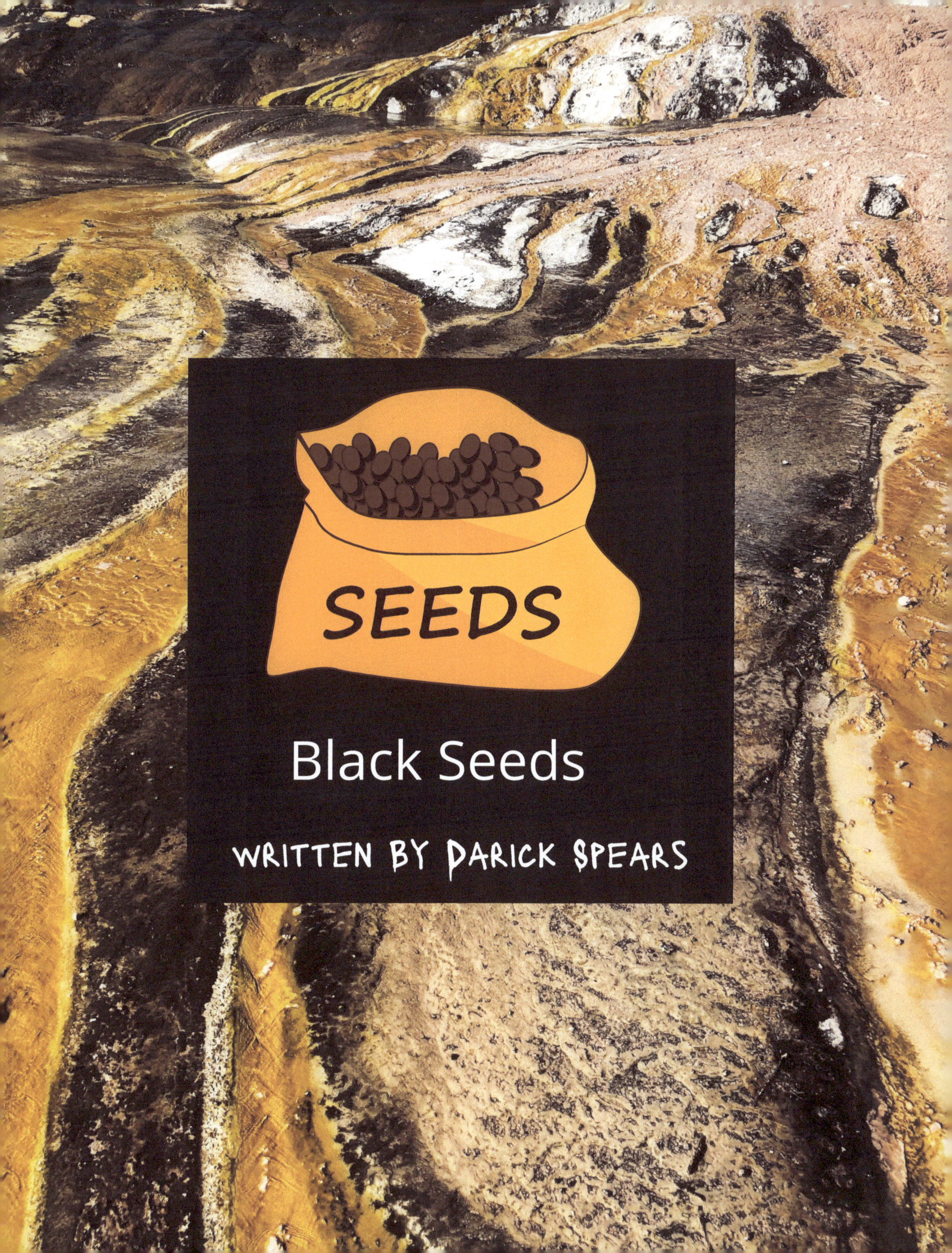
SEEDS
Black Seeds
WRITTEN BY DARICK SPEARS

Darick Books

THE FIRST BOOKSTORE OF ITS KIND

www.ingramcontent.com/pod-product-compliance
Lightning Source LLC
LaVergne TN
LVHW070225110826
845147LV00003B/651

* 9 7 8 1 9 5 4 1 3 3 1 2 9 *